THE EUCHARIST
IN SCRIPTURE

Catherine Upchurch

Little Rock
Scripture Study

A ministry of the Diocese of Little Rock
in partnership with Liturgical Press

Dear Friends in Christ,

Sacred Scripture is a wealth of inspired wisdom express-
ing Christian truths which challenge us to deepen our
relationship with God. Although the Bible can be intimi-
dating, it is important that we study God's word in the
Scriptures, because it is the basis of our faith and offers us
the thoughts and experiences of Christians past and
present. It is God speaking to us through the insights of
Church fathers and later saints.

I am pleased to present this study guide from Little Rock
Scripture Study to serve as an aid for reflection and con-
templation in your reading of Scripture. At the same time,
the guide will give you insight into how to apply what you
have read to your life today.

I encourage you to read Sacred Scripture slowly and
reflectively so that it can penetrate your heart and mind.
It is my hope that the Word of God will empower you as
Christians to live a life worthy of your call as a child of God
and a member of the body of Christ.

Sincerely in Christ,

✝ Anthony B. Taylor
Bishop of Little Rock

Sacred Scripture

"The Church has always venerated the divine Scriptures just as she venerates the body of the Lord, since from the table of both the word of God and of the body of Christ she unceasingly receives and offers to the faithful the bread of life, especially in the sacred liturgy. She has always regarded the Scriptures together with sacred tradition as the supreme rule of faith, and will ever do so. For, inspired by God and committed once and for all to writing, they impart the word of God Himself without change, and make the voice of the Holy Spirit resound in the words of the prophets and apostles. Therefore, like the Christian religion itself, all the preaching of the Church must be nourished and ruled by sacred Scripture. For in the sacred books, the Father who is in heaven meets His children with great love and speaks with them; and the force and power in the word of God is so great that it remains the support and energy of the Church, the strength of faith for her sons, the food of the soul, the pure and perennial source of spiritual life."

Vatican II, Dogmatic Constitution on Divine Revelation, no. 21.

INTERPRETATION OF SACRED SCRIPTURE

"Since God speaks in sacred Scripture through men in human fashion, the interpreter of sacred Scripture, in order to see clearly what God wanted to communicate to us, should carefully investigate what meaning the sacred writers really intended, and what God wanted to manifest by means of their words.

"Those who search out the intention of the sacred writers must, among other things, have regard for 'literary forms.' For truth is proposed and expressed in a variety of ways, depending on whether a text is history of one kind or another, or whether its form is that of prophecy, poetry, or some other type of speech. The interpreter must investigate what meaning the sacred writer intended to express and actually expressed in particular circumstances as he used contemporary literary forms in accordance with the situation of his own time and culture.

For the correct understanding of what the sacred author wanted to assert, due attention must be paid to the customary and characteristic styles of perceiving, speaking, and narrating which prevailed at the time of the sacred writer, and to the customs men normally followed in that period in their everyday dealings with one another."

Vatican II, Dogmatic Constitution on Divine Revelation, no. 12.

Instructions

MATERIALS FOR THE STUDY

This Study Guide: *The Eucharist in Scripture*

Commentary: *Welcome to the Feast: The Story of the Eucharist in Scripture*, by Clifford M. Yeary (Liturgical Press, 2014), is used with this study. The assigned pages are found at the beginning of each lesson.

Bible: We highly recommend the *Little Rock Catholic Study Bible* (Liturgical Press), although any version of the New American Bible, Revised Edition (NABRE), or the New Jerusalem Bible will suffice. Paraphrased editions are discouraged as they offer little, if any, help when facing difficult textual questions. Choose a Bible you feel free to write in or underline.

WEEKLY LESSONS

Lesson 1—Introduction; Some Old Testament Feasts with God
Lesson 2—A Wedding Feast in the Kingdom of God
Lesson 3—The Last Supper
Lesson 4—The Eucharist in Paul and Acts
Lesson 5—The Eucharist and John's Gospel

YOUR DAILY PERSONAL STUDY

The first step is prayer. Open your heart and mind to God. Reading Scripture is an opportunity to listen to God who loves you. Pray that the same Holy Spirit who guided the formation of Scripture will inspire you to correctly understand what you read and empower you to make what you read a part of your life.

The next step is commitment. Daily spiritual food is as necessary as food for the body. This study is divided into daily units. Schedule a regular time and place for your study, as free from distractions as possible. Allow about twenty minutes a day. Make it a daily appointment with God.

As you begin each lesson read the indicated pages of the commentary and the appropriate Scripture passages where indicated. This preparation will give you an overview of the entire lesson and help you to appreciate the context of individual passages.

As you reflect on Scripture, ask yourself these four questions:

1. *What does the Scripture passage say?*
   Read the passage slowly and reflectively. Use your imagination to picture the scene or enter into it.

2. *What does the Scripture passage mean?*
   Read the footnotes and the commentary to help you understand what the sacred writers intended and what God wanted to communicate by means of their words.

3. *What does the Scripture passage mean to me?*
   Meditate on the passage. God's Word is living and powerful. What is God saying to you today? How does the Scripture passage apply to your life today?

4. *What am I going to do about it?*
   Try to discover how God may be challenging you in this passage. An encounter with God contains a challenge to know God's will and follow it more closely in daily life.

THE QUESTIONS ASSIGNED FOR EACH DAY

Read the questions and references for each day. The questions are designed to help you listen to God's Word and to prepare you for the weekly small-group discussion.

Some of the questions can be answered briefly and objectively by referring to the Bible references and the commentary *(What does the passage say?)*. Some will lead you to a better understanding of how the Scriptures apply to the church, sacraments, and society *(What does the passage mean?)*. Some questions will invite you to consider how God's Word challenges or supports you in your relationships with God and others *(What does the passage mean to me?)*. Finally, the questions will lead you to examine your actions in light of Scripture *(What am I going to do about it?)*.

Write your responses in this study guide or in a notebook to help you clarify and organize your thoughts and feelings.

THE WEEKLY SMALL-GROUP MEETING

The weekly small-group sharing is the heart of the Little Rock Scripture Study Program. Participants gather in small groups to share the results of praying, reading, and reflecting on Scripture and on the assigned questions. The goal of the discussion is for group members to be strengthened and nourished individually and as a community through sharing how God's Word speaks to them and affects their daily lives. The daily study questions will guide the discussion; it is not necessary to discuss all the questions.

All members share the responsibility of creating an atmosphere of loving support and trust in the group by respecting the opinions and experiences of others, and by affirming and encouraging one another. The simple shared prayer that begins and ends each small group meeting also helps create the open and trusting environment in which group members can share their faith deeply and grow in the study of God's Word.

A distinctive feature of this program is its emphasis on and trust in God's presence working in and through each member. Sharing responses to God's presence in the Word and in others can bring about remarkable growth and transformation.

THE WRAP-UP LECTURE

The lecture is designed to develop and clarify the themes of each lesson. It is not intended to be the focus of the group's discussion. For this reason, the lecture always occurs *after* the small group discussion. If several small groups meet at one time, the groups may gather in a central location to listen to the lecture.

Lectures may be presented by a local speaker. They are also available in audio form on CD, and in visual form on DVD.

Introduction; Some Old Testament Feasts with God

WELCOME TO THE FEAST, PAGES I–18

Selected passages from Genesis, Exodus, and Isaiah

Day I

1. As you begin this study of *The Eucharist in Scripture*, what expectations or hopes do you bring with you?

2. In your experience, why do meals have the ability to create deep bonds among those who share them?

3. To reflect on the story of the Eucharist in Scripture, why begin with the Old Testament?

Day 2

Genesis 18:1-15

4. a) What can you imagine about the conditions of arid lands in the ancient world that might have made hospitality such a prized value in that region?

   b) What impresses you about the level of hospitality that Abraham and Sarah undertake for their three visitors (Gen 18:4-8)?

5. Is the presence of the three figures at the tent of Abraham and Sarah an early indication of the understanding of God as the Trinity (Gen 18:1-2)?

6. What are some early indicators in Genesis 18:1-15 that tell us the encounter with the three visitors is a divine encounter?

Day 3

7. In what ways have deeply meaningful meals or the sharing of food helped to whet your appetite for the meal that Christ offers in the Eucharist? Is this a new idea for you, or is this something that you have experienced?

8. Both Sarah and Abraham laugh at the news of Sarah's upcoming pregnancy (Gen 18:12; see also 17:15-17). Where is the response to their laughter, "Is anything too marvelous for the LORD to do?" echoed in the New Testament (see Luke 1:36-37) and what connections might we make?

9. The canticle of Zechariah (Luke 1:68-79) is part of the church's Morning Prayer as a reminder of God's promise of salvation from the time of Abraham to the present. How can these words of prayer help to shape our expectations for the day ahead and for our lives in general?

Day 4

Exodus 12:1-30

10. What historical event is commemorated in the Passover meal, and why is it celebrated as the "head of the calendar" in every generation of Jews (Exod 12:11-13, 24-27)? (See Exod 13:6-10.)

11. What two feasts are combined to create the Passover as described in Exodus 12?

12. In Israel's history the celebration of Passover took on greater and greater significance over time (e.g., Deut 16:1-4) and after times when it had been neglected, it was restored with fervor (e.g., 2 Chr 34–35). What do these developments indicate to you about the importance of the Passover meal?

Day 5

13. In what way could Jesus' journey to Jerusalem (Luke 9:28-31) be understood as an "exodus"?

Isaiah 25:6-10b

14. Describe the general historical background for the prophecy found in Isaiah 25.

15. Why would the description of a feast hosted by the LORD of hosts be both ironic and hopeful in that time of Judah's history?

Day 6

Isaiah 55:1-5

16. The descriptions of the feasts in Isaiah 25 (above) and in Isaiah 55 come from different time periods in Judah's history, but they both have apocalyptic overtones. What does this mean?

17. What is the condition that will allow God's people to come to the divine feast (Isa 55:3)?

18. The prophet recalls how David was a witness to the people, but now indicates that all will serve as witnesses and "summon a nation you knew not" (Isa 55:4-5). How important is it in your parish that you give witness even to those outside of the faith, inviting them to the feast that God sets for us?

A Wedding Feast in the Kingdom of God

WELCOME TO THE FEAST, PAGES 19–34

Selected passages from Isaiah and the gospels

Day 1

1. Before moving into this lesson, are there any particular insights from Lesson One that were helpful to you? Why?

Isaiah 54:4-8; 62:5

2. The imagery of bride and bridegroom is used in Scripture to speak of God's relationship with his people. (As examples, see Jer 2:2; Ezek 16:8-14; Hos 2:21-22.) What is one of the major differences between the way the image is used in Isaiah 54:4-8 and the way it is used in Isaiah 62:5?

3. Why would a general knowledge of wedding feasts and messianic expectations be an important part of appreciating the feast as a sign of the Messiah? (See Hos 2:21-22; Matt 22:1-14; Rev 19:7-9.)

Day 2

John 2:1-11; 3:25-30

4. In the scene at the wedding in Cana, what kinds of connections can be made between the wine and Jesus' hour (John 2:1-11)? (See Amos 9:13; Jer 31:11-12; John 5:25-29; 7:6-8; 12:23; 17:1-5.)

5. Why is it significant that John the Baptist refers to Jesus as the "bridegroom" (John 3:29)? (See Rev 19:6-9; 21:2-4.)

6. How does the image of the church as the bride and Christ as the bridegroom help you to appreciate the kind of relationship we are being offered (John 3:29)? (See 2 Cor 11:2; Eph 5:29-31.)

Day 3

7. How do you understand Jesus' response to those who question why his followers do not fast (Matt 9:14-15; Mark 2:19-20; Luke 5:34-35)?

8. If you were to use fasting and feasting as symbolic of your spiritual life, which of the two characterizes your journey at this time?

Luke 13:23-30

9. What is the connection between sharing a meal with Jesus and the condition of one's soul (Luke 13:23-30)? And why do we sometimes mistakenly think that sharing such a meal requires purity?

Day 4

Mark 6:31-45; 8:1-9

10. a) What is the root meaning of the word "Eucharist"?

   b) Why would it be acceptable, even important, to recognize the eucharistic elements in some of the meals Jesus shared with his followers even before the Last Supper?

11. What connections with the Old Testament are made in the way Mark sets up his first account of Jesus feeding the multitude (Mark 6:31-45)? (See Exod 18:21-25; Num 27:16-17; Ps 23; Ezek 34:15.)

12. Mark's original audience would have heard the story of Jesus, and the particular stories of these feedings, by listening within a community that was a mixture of Jews and Gentiles. These factors would have influenced the way Mark told the stories and the way they were heard. How aware are you of the factors that affect your own hearing of these stories in your particular location?

Day 5

13. How does the blessing pronounced by Jesus differ in Mark's two accounts of the multiplication (Mark 6:41; 8:7)?

14. Why is it significant that Jesus invited his followers to gather the food and distribute it once it was blessed (Mark 6:37-38, 41; 8:4-7)?

15. In between Mark's two accounts of the multiplication of loaves, what does Jesus do that indicates a shift from a Jewish to a Gentile audience (Mark 7:1-23)?

Day 6

16. How does Mark use the story of the encounter between Jesus and the Syrophoenician (Gentile) woman to further set the stage for the mission to the Gentiles that the church would eventually take up (Mark 7:24-30)?

17. Review the chart on page 30 of the commentary comparing the two accounts in Mark's gospel. What differences and similarities stand out to you, and why?

18. In four of the accounts of the feeding of the multitudes, it is noted that Jesus is moved with pity for the crowds (Matt 14:14; 15:32; Mark 6:34; 8:2). His compassion is not just a feeling but moves him to action on their behalf. How do you see compassionate action happening in your parish in imitation of Jesus?

The Last Supper

WELCOME TO THE FEAST, PAGES 35–53

Selected passages from Isaiah, the Synoptic Gospels, and 1 Corinthians

Day 1

1. In your discussion of the previous lesson, what insight did you gather from the contribution of others in your group?

Mark 8:22-26, 27-30

2. Scholars sometimes refer to the "Markan sandwich" to describe a writing technique used by the evangelist (illustrated briefly in Mark 8). How would you describe this and how might it differ from typical storytelling in our day?

3. Why is Jesus' identity as the Messiah a point of concern in Mark 8:27-31?

Day 2

4. What insights in the commentary about Jewish festive meals help you to appreciate the spiritual and religious sensibilities of the early followers of Jesus?

5. Given what we know about the prescribed foods and script of a Passover meal, why would the gospel writers who tell the story of the Last Supper not include those details if there is indeed a Passover connection?

Matthew 26:26-29; *Mark* 14:22-25

6. In the Last Supper accounts, the gospels of Matthew (26:26) and Mark (14:22) differ from Luke (22:19) and Paul (1 Cor 11:24) in their use of the Greek terms for blessing and giving thanks. In your experience, how are the ideas of blessing and giving thanks connected?

Day 3

7. In your own words, summarize the general differences in perspective found in the gospels of Mark and of Matthew. (In addition to the commentary for this course, the introduction to each gospel in your Bible may also offer helpful information.)

8. Compare what Jesus does with the bread in the gospel accounts of the Last Supper (Matt 26:26; Mark 14:22; Luke 22:19) with the actions found in the feeding of the multitude earlier in the gospels. How do taking, blessing, breaking, and giving become not only the actions of our celebrations of Eucharist but a way of living that reveals God's presence?

9. What might be the reason(s) that only in Matthew does Jesus refer to the kingdom of heaven while in the other gospels he refers to the kingdom of God?

Day 4

10. What is significant about what Matthew adds to Mark's narrative of Jesus identifying the wine and sharing it with his disciples (Matt 26:27-29; Mark 14:23-25)?

11. What phrase appears in Matthew 26:28 to indicate a theology of expiation? And what does that mean? (See Exod 24:6-8; Rom 3:23-25; Heb 10:11-12.)

12. What could have been meant in the original languages and cultures of the Bible to help us understand the intention of Jesus shedding his blood "for many" (Mark 14:24) or "on behalf of many" (Matt 26:28)? (See Isa 52:13-15; 53:11-12.)

Day 5

Luke 22:14-34; *Luke* 24:13-35

13. The Last Supper account in Luke 22:15-20 can be characterized as part of a farewell discourse for Jesus' closest followers (see 22:14-34). If you knew you had time to say good-bye to those closest to you, what message would you want to impart?

14. One theme that emerges in Luke's version of Jesus' farewell to his disciples is that of humility and greatness (Luke 22:24-30). How do you understand these virtues and why is it important in our spiritual journey to have a proper sense of both virtues? (To help with your reflection, see Ps 25:9; Matt 20:20-28; Phil 2:5-8; 1 Pet 2:9-10.)

15. In Luke's gospel Jesus articulates a desire to share the Passover meal with his followers (Luke 22:15). Page through the Gospel of Luke and identify a few other places where table fellowship was important as Jesus formed his followers.

Day 6

16. Luke 22:20 and 1 Corinthians 11:25 both speak of the cup of the new covenant. What emphasis is being surfaced by noting a "new" covenant?

Luke 24:13-35

17. Luke makes special note of the presence of Jesus' betrayer at the Last Supper (Luke 22:21) and in the Emmaus account the presence of the disillusioned at a meal with eucharistic overtones (Luke 24:13-35). Are there any lessons for you or your parish as you consider the role of the Eucharist as an instrument of healing or instruction?

18. Read through the Emmaus account in Luke 24:13-35. When have you felt empowered as a disciple by celebrating the Eucharist? Try to identify one or two times that you felt moved to action of some kind as a result.

The Eucharist in Paul and Acts

WELCOME TO THE FEAST, PAGES 54–70

Selected passages from Acts of the Apostles, Galatians, and 1 Corinthians

Day 1

1. In the previous lesson, we learned that the Last Supper accounts are similar in the Synoptic Gospels (Matthew, Mark, and Luke) and in Paul's First Letter to the Corinthians. This tells us something about how the early church treated its most important traditions. How do your own efforts to pass on the gift of Jesus' presence with us demonstrate its importance?

Acts 2:38-47

2. Create a list of the features that characterized the early church in the time immediately following the resurrection and Pentecost (Acts 2:42-47). If you were to create a listing for your own parish community, in what ways would it be similar and in what ways different from Acts?

3. What might be the reason that breaking of bread is mentioned twice in Acts 2:42-47?

Day 2

4. Why did the growing number of Gentile believers pose particular challenges to the way the early Christian communities would celebrate Eucharist (Acts 10:9-16, 34, 44-49; 11:1-3)?

Acts 11:19-26

5. Do you think most Christians have an awareness of the Jewish identity of the earliest followers, or the tensions that would have been quite real as the communities became more and more Gentile? (See Acts 10:45-49; 11:19-26.) How might such an awareness help us when tensions arise in our communities today?

Acts 15:1-12; *Galatians* 2:11-14

6. Paul and Peter and Barnabas were instrumental in helping the early community of believers accept the conversion of the Gentiles (Acts 15:1-12). However, in the practical application of bringing Gentiles and Jews together for Eucharist they were divided. What can you determine about how each evangelist tried to resolve the turmoil (Gal 1:11-14; 2:7-9, 11-14)?

Day 3

Romans 14:13-23; *1 Corinthians* 10:16-31

7. What could account for Paul taking two different approaches to the issue of consuming meat sacrificed to idols? (See Rom 14:13-23; 1 Cor 10:18-21.)

8. a) What is the "cup of blessing" in the Passover and festive meals of Israel (recall chart on page 40 of commentary)? (See Matt 26:27-28; Mark 14:23-24; Luke 22:20.)

   b) Why is the "cup of blessing" then referred to as one we bless in 1 Corinthians 10:16?

9. How can the Greek term *koinonia* be translated? (See 1 Cor 10:16; 1:9.)

Day 4

10. What does Paul teach the Corinthians about the effects of drinking the cup and eating the bread in Eucharist (1 Cor 10:16-21; 1 Cor 1:4-9)?

11. Locate Corinth on a map depicting the time of the early church (online or in your Bible). How would its location and commercial convenience have made it an important place for Christianity?

12. What was the population like in Corinth at the time of Paul?

Day 5

13. Archaeological findings at Corinth reveal some features of houses of the early Christian era. What kind of space would a "church" have had for their members to gather and celebrate Eucharist?

14. What is more surprising to you, to learn that in the early centuries the Eucharist was celebrated as part of a larger meal called an *agape* or love feast (1 Cor 11:18-21; Jude v. 12) or to learn that the Eucharist was celebrated in homes (Rom 16:3-5; 1 Cor 16:19; Col 4:15)?

15. The intimacy of sharing a meal in a home is one aspect of Eucharist as presented in the Bible that is sometimes hard to recapture in our large or mobile parishes. How does your parish try to highlight this aspect of the Sunday Eucharist?

Day 6

1 Corinthians 11:17-34

16. a) Why does Paul tell the church in Corinth that their meetings "are doing more harm than good" (1 Cor 11:17)? (See 1:10.)

    b) While our parishes may not have the precise problems as those outlined in ancient Corinth, what challenges do we face to ensure that our celebrations do more good than harm?

17. What in Paul's argument (1 Cor 11:23-31) would be most convincing to you in a community that misses the significance of sharing in Christ's body?

Acts 20:7-12; 27:27-36

18. Luke and Paul make use of eucharistic language and images even in passages not directly related to sharing the Eucharist itself. This technique heightens their audience's appreciation for God's many ways of offering nourishment. Where have you seen or heard eucharistic references outside of Mass that catch your attention and feed your religious imagination?

The Eucharist and John's Gospel

WELCOME TO THE FEAST, PAGES 71–87

Selected passages from the Gospel of John

Day 1

1. Did anything surface in the discussion or lecture from last week's lesson that you are still pondering in some way? If so, share this with your group.

2. Summarize the possible reasons that John did not include in his gospel an account of the Last Supper that includes the institution of the Eucharist.

3. Look through the sixth chapter of John to situate yourself in the way John will develop his theology of Eucharist. Before moving into the material in detail, what impresses you about the way the evangelists were able to craft their materials? Do you have a growing appreciation for the way God used (and continues to use) individual talents and experiences to promote the kingdom of God?

Day 2

John 6:1-15

4. What subtle and important connections are being made in the multiplication scene by noting that Jesus went up a mountain (John 6:3), the Passover was near (6:4), and the abundant grass of the location (6:10)?

5. "Gather the fragments left over, so that nothing will be wasted" (John 6:12). What experiences of abundance have helped you appreciate God's generosity and God's invitation to become a more generous person yourself?

John 6:16-21

6. When has knowing who Jesus is in your life helped you to give over your fears and trust in his presence (John 6:20-21)?

Day 3

John 6:22-59

7. In the opening verses of the bread of life discourse (John 6:22-31) what clues do we have that the crowds do not yet understand the purpose of the earlier multiplication of food, and do not yet understand who Jesus is?

8. What is significant about the reference to the "bread from heaven" that God's people ate in the desert (6:31-32)? (See Exod 16:33; Deut 8:15-20; Wis 16:20-21.)

9. When Jesus tells the crowd that he will give them bread from heaven (John 6:32-33) and that he is himself the Bread of Life (6:35, 48-51), they are naturally confused. But he has been leading them to this greater understanding all along. What example can you give from your own life that demonstrates how powerfully our preconceived ideas or limited imaginations can make us resistant to truth?

Day 4

10. Prayerfully read John 6:51, repeating it aloud or silently as you ponder its meaning. At this time in your life, what phrase of just a few words in this sentence continues to feed you in some way? What might be drawing you to this particular phrase?

11. What historical tensions at the time of John's writing (late first century) might help to explain the graphic nature of the words from Jesus about eating his flesh and drinking his blood (John 6:52-58)?

12. What are some ways that your parish teaches in word and deed the truth that "the one who feeds on me will have life because of me" (John 6:57)?

Day 5

John 6:60-71

13. It can be a common assumption that the early church emerged somewhat uniform in its beliefs and practices. However, the biblical evidence shows that at the time of Jesus and during the time of the apostles there were rocky times and even times of division (e.g., John 6:60-66). What can account for the strength of this small community of believers that would one day expand across the globe?

14. Consider how Peter responded to Jesus' question about whether they wanted to leave (John 6:69). When confronted with internal doubts, or by those who cannot understand your devotion to Christ in a world that seems quite broken, what is your response?

John 21:1-14

15. Consider that in John 21:1-14, the risen Jesus appears to his followers through an early morning meal on the seashore. What does it tell you about the importance of a meal, a meal with Jesus, and a meal that communicates his real presence that he would reveal his resurrection in this way?

Day 6

16. Having come to the end of this exploration of the Eucharist in various biblical accounts, what one or two insights were either most surprising to you or most helpful to you?

17. When you participate in your parish celebrations of Eucharist, how can you better prepare yourself to receive Jesus who nourishes us in the words of Scripture and in his body and blood?

18. Consider one or two practical ways that you can witness to the reality of God's gift to us in the Eucharist. What might you be willing to do even in small but deliberate ways?

ABBREVIATIONS

Books of the Bible

Gen—Genesis
Exod—Exodus
Lev—Leviticus
Num—Numbers
Deut—Deuteronomy
Josh—Joshua
Judg—Judges
Ruth—Ruth
1 Sam—1 Samuel
2 Sam—2 Samuel
1 Kgs—1 Kings
2 Kgs—2 Kings
1 Chr—1 Chronicles
2 Chr—2 Chronicles
Ezra—Ezra
Neh—Nehemiah
Tob—Tobit
Jdt—Judith
Esth—Esther
1 Macc—1 Maccabees
2 Macc—2 Maccabees
Job—Job
Ps(s)—Psalm(s)
Prov—Proverbs
Eccl—Ecclesiastes
Song—Song of Songs
Wis—Wisdom
Sir—Sirach
Isa—Isaiah
Jer—Jeremiah
Lam—Lamentations
Bar—Baruch
Ezek—Ezekiel
Dan—Daniel
Hos—Hosea
Joel—Joel
Amos—Amos

Obad—Obadiah
Jonah—Jonah
Mic—Micah
Nah—Nahum
Hab—Habakkuk
Zeph—Zephaniah
Hag—Haggai
Zech—Zechariah
Mal—Malachi
Matt—Matthew
Mark—Mark
Luke—Luke
John—John
Acts—Acts
Rom—Romans
1 Cor—1 Corinthians
2 Cor—2 Corinthians
Gal—Galatians
Eph—Ephesians
Phil—Philippians
Col—Colossians
1 Thess—1 Thessalonians
2 Thess—2 Thessalonians
1 Tim—1 Timothy
2 Tim—2 Timothy
Titus—Titus
Phlm—Philemon
Heb—Hebrews
Jas—James
1 Pet—1 Peter
2 Pet—2 Peter
1 John—1 John
2 John—2 John
3 John—3 John
Jude—Jude
Rev—Revelation

NOTES